gr. 4-8

HOW TO DRAW
FANTASY
CASTLES

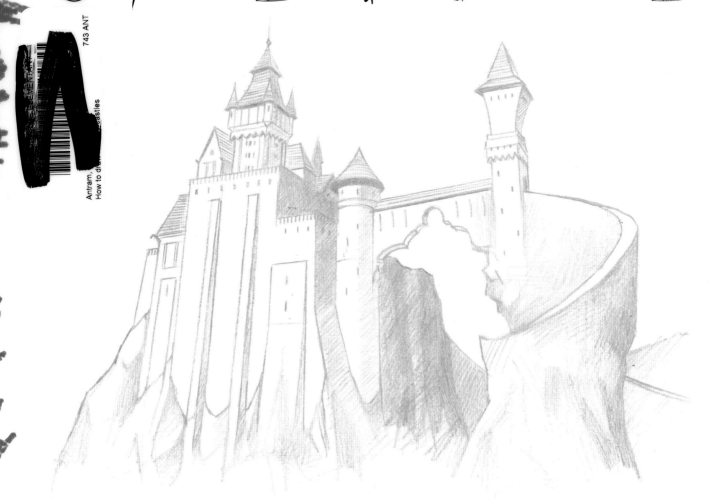

David Antram

PowerKiDS
press™

New York

Published in 2012 by The Rosen Publishing Group, Inc.
29 East 21st Street, New York, NY 10010

Editor: Rob Walker
U.S. Editor: Kara Murray

Library of Congress Cataloging-in-Publication Data

Antram, David, 1958-
 Fantasy castles / by David Antram. — 1st ed.
    p. cm. — (How to draw)
 ISBN 978-1-4488-6461-4 (library binding) —
ISBN 978-1-4488-6467-6 (pbk.) —
ISBN 978-1-4488-6468-3 (6-pack)
1. Fantasy in art—Juvenile literature. 2. Castles in art—Juvenile literature. 3. Drawing—Technique—Juvenile literature. I. Title.

NC825.F25A58 2012
743'.87--dc22

2011017644

Manufactured in China

CPSIA Compliance Information: Batch #SW2102PK:
For Further Information contact Rosen Publishing,
New York, New York at 1-800-237-9932

PAPER FROM
SUSTAINABLE
FORESTS

Contents

Making a Start

Learning to draw is about looking and seeing. Keep practicing and get to know your subject. Use a sketchbook to make quick drawings. Start by doodling and experimenting with shapes and patterns. There are many ways to draw. This book shows only some methods. Visit art galleries, look at artists' drawings, see how friends draw, but above all, find your own way.

Remember that practice makes perfect. If it
looks wrong, start again. Keep working at it.
The more you draw, the more you will learn.

5

Drawing Tools

Here are just a few of the many tools that you can use for drawing. Let your imagination go and have fun experimenting with all the different marks you can make.

Pencil

Watercolor pencil

Charcoal pencil

Charcoal stick

Pastels

Finger painting

Black, gray, and white pastel on gray construction paper

Each grade of **pencil** makes a different mark, from fine, gray lines to soft, black ones. Hard pencils are graded as #2 1/2, #3, and #4 (the hardest). A #2 pencil is ideal for general sketching. A soft pencil is a #1 pencil. It makes the softest, blackest line.

Watercolor pencils come in many different colors and make a line similar to a #2 pencil. But paint over your finished drawing with clean water, and the lines will soften and run.

It is less messy and easier to achieve a fine line with a **charcoal pencil** than a stick of charcoal. Create soft tones by smudging lines with your finger. **Ask an adult** to spray the drawing with fixative to prevent further smudging.

Pastels are brittle sticks of powdered color. They blend and smudge easily and are ideal for quick sketches. Pastel drawings work well on textured, colored paper. **Ask an adult** to spray your finished drawing with fixative.

Experiment with **finger painting**. Your fingerprints make exciting patterns and textures. Use your fingers to smudge soft pencil, charcoal, and pastel lines.

Ballpoint pens are very useful for sketching and making notes. Make different tones by building up layers of shading.

A **mapping pen** has to be dipped into bottled ink to fill the nib. Different nib shapes make different marks. Try putting a diluted ink wash over parts of the finished drawing.

Draftsmen's pens and specialist **art pens** can produce extremely fine lines and are ideal for creating surface texture. A variety of pen nibs are available that produce different widths of line.

Felt—tip pens are ideal for quick sketches. If the ink is not waterproof, try drawing on wet paper and see what happens.

Broad—nibbed **marker pens** make interesting lines and are good for large, bold sketches. Try using a black pen for the main sketch and a gray one to block in areas of shadow.

Paintbrushes are shaped differently to make different marks. Japanese brushes are soft and produce beautiful flowing lines. Large sable brushes are good for painting a wash over a line drawing. Fine brushes are good for drawing delicate lines.

Ballpoint pen

Mapping pen

Draftsman's pen

Felt—tip pen

Marker pen

Paintbrush

7

Materials

Try using different types of drawing paper and materials. Experiment with charcoal, wax crayons, and pastels. All pens, from felt-tips to ballpoints, will make interesting marks. You could also try drawing with pen and ink on wet paper.

Ink silhouette

Silhouette is a style of drawing that mainly uses solid black shapes.

Felt-tips come in a range of line widths. The wider pens are good for filling in large areas of flat tone.

Lines drawn in **ink** cannot be erased, so keep your ink drawings sketchy and less rigid. Don't worry about mistakes as these lines can be lost in the drawing as it develops.

Adding light and shade to a drawing with an ink pen can be tricky. Use a solid layer of ink for the very darkest areas and cross-hatching (straight lines crisscrossing each other) for ordinary dark tones. Hatching (straight lines running parallel to each other) can be used for midrange tones. Leave the lightest areas white.

Cross-hatching

Hatching

Pencil drawings can include a vast amount of detail and tone. Try experimenting with different grades of pencil to get a range of light and shade effects in your drawing.

Remember: the best equipment and materials will not necessarily make the best drawing. Only practice will.

Perspective

If you look at any object from different viewpoints, you will see that the part that is closest to you looks larger and the part farthest away from you looks smaller. Drawing in perspective is a way of creating a feeling of space, or of showing three dimensionson a flat surface.

V.P.

The vanishing point (V.P.) is the place in a perspective drawing where parallel lines appear to meet. The position of the vanishing point depends on the viewer's eye level. Sometimes a low viewpoint can give your drawing added drama.

Two-point perspective uses two
vanishing points: one for lines
running along the length of the
object and one on the opposite side
for lines running across the width
of the object.

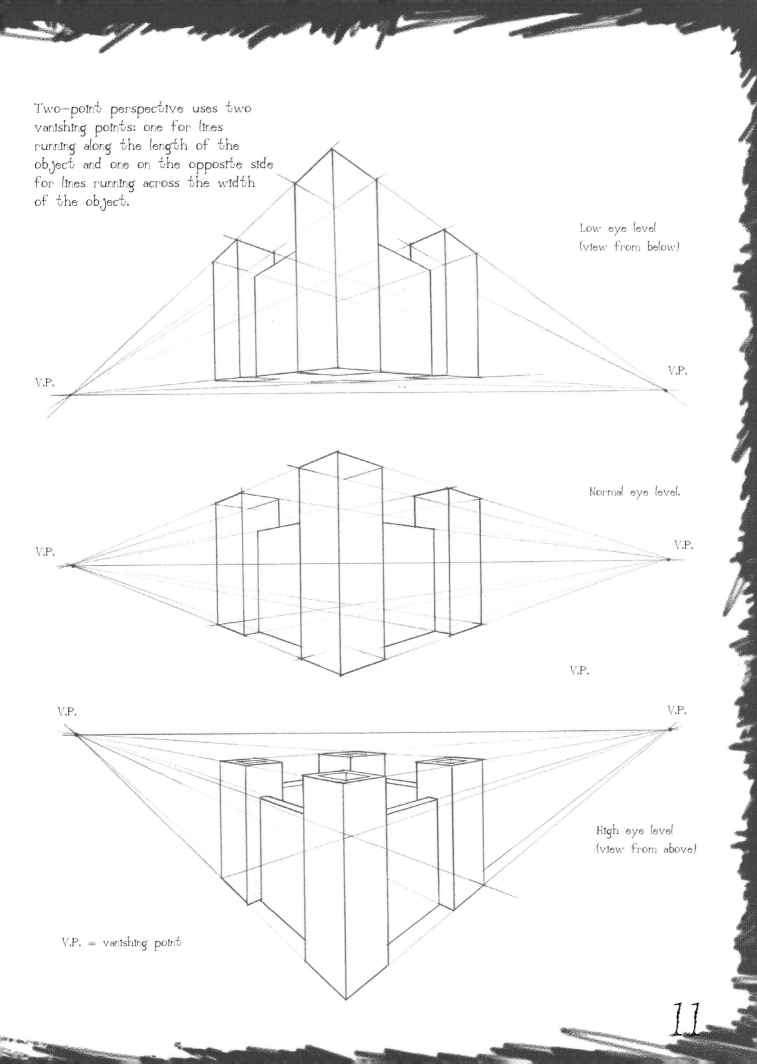

Low eye level
(view from below)

V.P.

V.P.

Normal eye level.

V.P.

V.P.

V.P.

V.P.

V.P.

High eye level
(view from above)

V.P. = vanishing point

11

Three-Point Perspective

Three-point perspective uses three vanishing points: one for lines running along the length of the object, one on the opposite side for lines running across the width of the object, and one above or below for lines running up or down the object. This gives a very realistic three-dimensional effect.

V.P.   V.P.

V.P.

V.P.

Low eye level
(view from below)

V.P.   V.P.

High eye level
(view from above)

V.P.   V.P.

V.P.

In this perspective drawing, you can see how each individual tower is created in perspective using the same vanishing points.

When you have finished your drawing, you can remove any unwanted construction lines created by using the vanishing points.

V.P.

Tips on Perspective

Drawing three-dimensional buildings relies heavily on perspective to get the correct proportions and make the drawing accurate. Here are some tips to help you with problems of perspective.

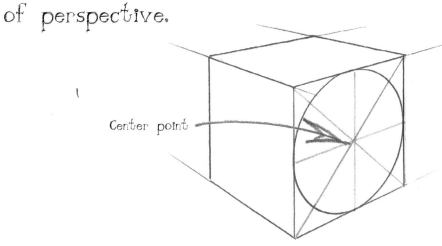

Center point

Dividing a square and circle in perspective:

After drawing a perspective box, draw straight lines from corner to corner. The exact center point is where they meet. When you've found the center point, you can divide the square or circle evenly.

To add windows evenly spaced along a wall:

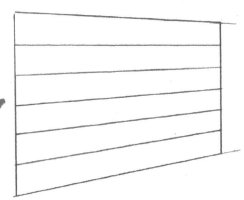

Divide the height of the wall evenly, then draw a straight line from corner to corner.

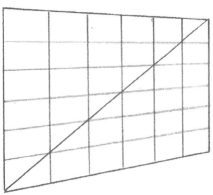

Your vertical points of division will be found where the diagonal line crosses the others.

Using these construction lines, add the windows, which will appear evenly spaced.

14

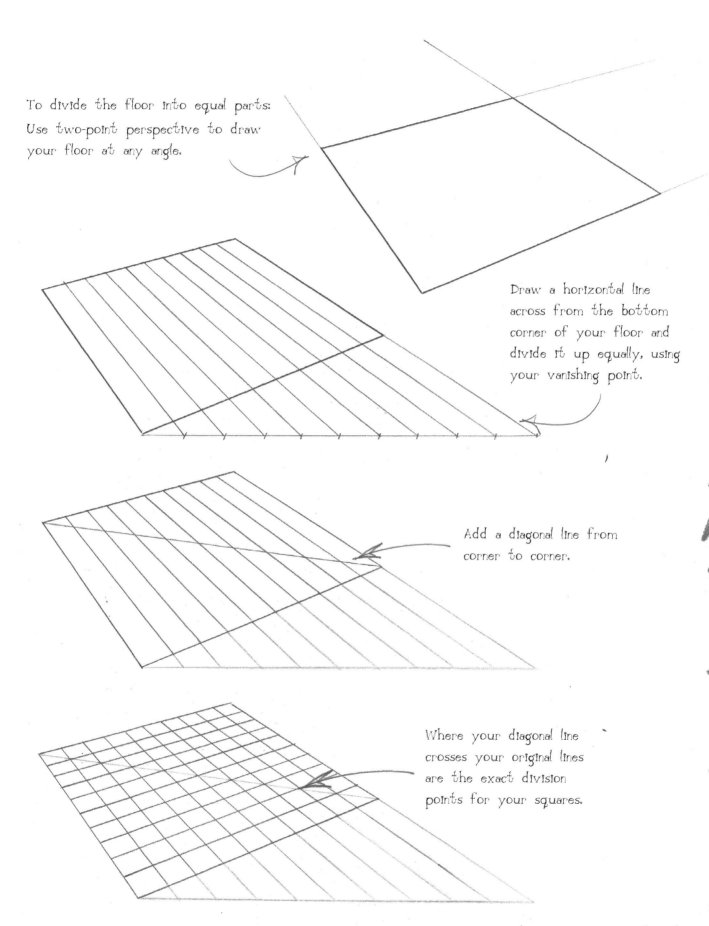

To divide the floor into equal parts:
Use two-point perspective to draw
your floor at any angle.

Draw a horizontal line
across from the bottom
corner of your floor and
divide it up equally, using
your vanishing point.

Add a diagonal line from
corner to corner.

Where your diagonal line
crosses your original lines
are the exact division
points for your squares.

15

Basic Castle

This basic castle makes good use of the perspective drawing techniques explained on the previous pages.

First draw a box in two-point perspective.

Using the grid technique (pages 14–15), map out the ground plan of the castle.

Use the grid and oval techniques for the cylindrical front towers.

Use the grid to draw rectangular rear towers.

Add top sections to each of the towers using the construction lines as a guide.

Draw straight lines joining the towers for the outer walls of the castle.

Add an arched gateway.

Draw curved lines for the roof tiles on the cylindrical towers.

Add the many details to the battlements at the top of each tower.

Add the windows.

Add a gate.

Remove any unwanted construction lines.

17

Underwater Castle

T his fantasy castle has been built underwater from parts of natural sea shells and coral.

Sketch in the towers of the castle.

Sketch in construction lines for the clam the castle sits in.

Add curved lines to the top of each tower to give them shape.

Sketch the wavy edge of the clamshell.

Add an edge of coral reef holding the clam.

Natural Shapes
This castle's walls are based on clamshells. Think what other parts of this castle could be adapted from marine life. Other fantasy castles can be inspired by different environments.

Start to sketch in the shape of the coral reef.

Start to add tone to the structures, depending on the light source.

Add more detail to define the shapes of the structures.

Draw lines down the clam to show the ridges in the shell.

Add small, dark windows and other details to the towers.

Add some fish.

Sketch in the shape of some coral that looks like a tree.

Draw many curved lines on the shell for its textured surface. These should match the shape of the wavy edge.

Shade in areas where light wouldn't reach.

Complete the fish details.

Add more detail to the coral tree and coral surface.

Remove any unwanted construction lines.

19

Dracula's Castle

Dracula's castle sits atop a craggy mountain, ominous and scary.

Start by using two-point perspective to draw the basic shapes of all the towers.

Draw construction lines for the top parts of the towers.

Adding Shade

In order to give your drawing a feeling of solidity, first decide what direction the light is coming from. Then shade areas where the light wouldn't reach. Use a light tone for areas that get a little light.

Start to add the mountain and the bridge.

Sketch in the basic structure for each of the windows.

Add structural design details to the towers.

Add the window frames.

Begin to add shade to the sides of the castle not getting much light.

Draw the roof tiles.

Add long lines curving down from the castle for the buttresses (wall supports).

Add dark shading for the windows.

Add a moon and some creepy bat silhouettes.

Add shade to the side of the building.

Draw lines for the texture of the mountain.

Remove any unwanted construction lines.

Ice Castle

This ice castle is made from jagged blocks of ice. Empress Anna of Russia created a real ice palace in St. Petersburg in the eighteenth century.

Start by drawing the outline shape of the ice castle.

Draw spiky lines around the main shape of the castle.

Add shading to areas where light wouldn't reach.

Shade in a doorway and draw a winding three-dimensional path.

Draw straight lines for the stairs.

Add dark shading for the windows.

Draw faint lines to look like shards of ice.

Add rocky detail to the base of the ice castle.

Sketch rough, jagged shapes for shards of ice.

Shade to add detail.

Draw reflections in the frozen lake.

Remove any unwanted construction lines.

23

Medieval Tower

T

his tall medieval tower is the perfect backdrop for a story of knights, princesses, and even dragons.

Start by drawing construction lines for the tower and its base.

Add a pointed turret to the top of the tower.

Use two-point perspective to help.

Draw a balcony on the side of the tower.

Add the arched shape of the doorway.

Draw pointed turret shapes.

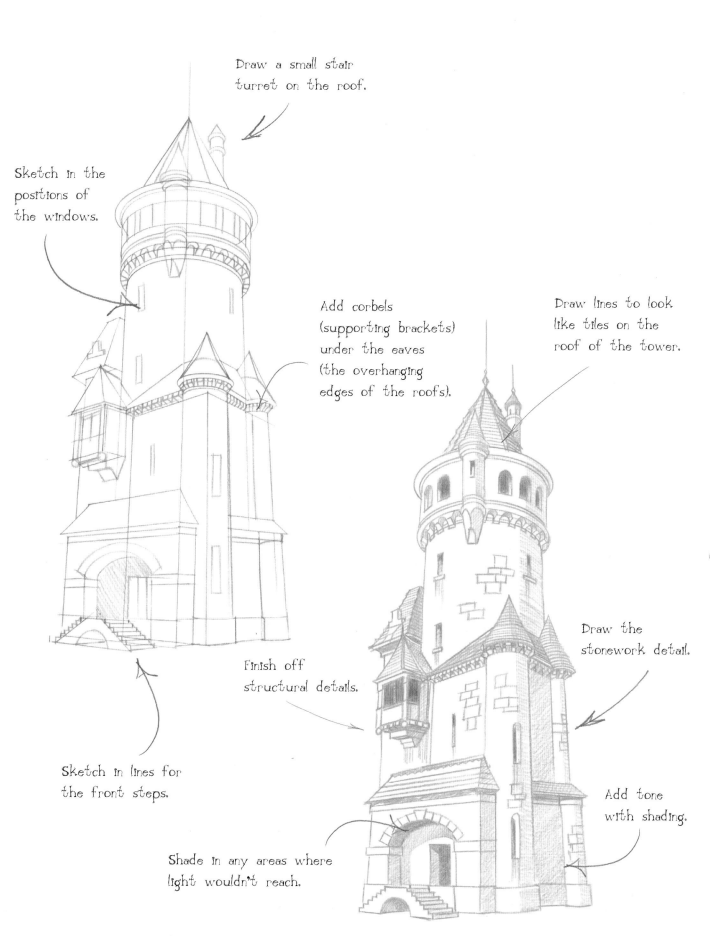

Draw a small stair turret on the roof.

Sketch in the positions of the windows.

Add corbels (supporting brackets) under the eaves (the overhanging edges of the roofs).

Draw lines to look like tiles on the roof of the tower.

Finish off structural details.

Sketch in lines for the front steps.

Draw the stonework detail.

Shade in any areas where light wouldn't reach.

Add tone with shading.

25

Cliff-Top Castle

This castle is built high up on the cliffs, which makes it very difficult for enemies to attack.

Start by drawing the construction lines for the basic shape of the castle.

Use two-point perspective to make the drawing look three-dimensional.

Draw a curved line for the cliff wall.

V.P.

Add points to the tops of the towers.

Add detail to the castle bridge.

Add a three-dimensional effect to the curved wall.

Add buttresses to the main tower.

Draw more
structural detail.

Mark the positions
of the windows.

Shade areas to
create tone.

Composition

By framing your drawing
with a square or a rectangle,
you can make it look
completely different.

Shade in the roof
using straight lines.

Finish drawing
structural detail.

Add cross-hatching
for tone.

Draw windows.

Shade to create a
rocky texture.

Shade in any areas
where light
wouldn't reach.

Remove any unwanted construction lines.

Pirate Skull Castle

Pirates live in this spooky castle made from a giant skull and bones. They shoot cannons at their enemies from the eyes and mouth.

Start by drawing a circle for the skull.

Sketch two large bone shapes behind the skull.

Add some curved lines to the tops of the bones.

Draw three rounded shapes for the eyes and nose.

Shade in the hollows of the eyes.

Sketch straight lines to create cheekbones.

Add doorways and sketch curved lines for staircases.

Position the mouth and shade it in.

Sketch in the pirates on
the tops of the bones.

Add shading to
areas where light
wouldn't reach.

Add detail to the nose
and cheekbones.

Draw a pirate flag and
add detail to the pirates.

Sketch in straight lines
for the staircases.

Add cross-hatching
to the nose.

Add shading to create tone.

Draw the uneven
shapes of the teeth.

Finish off the detail on the
staircases and doorways.

Add a rocky texture
on the ground.

Remove any unwanted
construction lines.

Fairy Tale Castle

This traditional castle is home to fairy tale princes and princesses. Its many turrets and tall towers give it a magical look.

Start by drawing construction lines for the basic shapes of the towers.

Use two-point perspective to make the castle look three-dimensional.

V.P.

Add pointed cones to the tops of the towers.

Using straight lines, draw step shapes along the tops of the main buildings.

Add detail to the castle towers.

Mark in the positions of the windows.

Add battlements.

Use horizontal lines to create the tiled tops of the towers.

Draw the arched detail of the windows.

Shade in areas where light would not reach.

Draw bushes using lots of little lines.

Shade the towers to look three-dimensional.

Shade the base of the castle to look like rock.

Remove any unwanted construction lines.

31

Glossary

composition (kom-puh-ZIH-shun) The arrangement of the parts of a picture.

construction lines (kun-STRUK-shun LYNZ) Guidelines used in the early stages of a drawing. They are usually erased later.

fixative (FIK-suh-tiv) A resin that can be sprayed onto a drawing to prevent smudging. It must only be used by an adult.

ground plan (GROWND PLAN) The space on the ground that is occupied by the floor of a building, also called a building's footprint.

perspective (per-SPEK-tiv) A method of drawing in which near objects are shown larger than faraway objects.

proportion (pruh-POR-shun) The correct relationship of scale between each part of the drawing.

silhouette (sih-luh-WET) A drawing that shows only a flat dark shape, like a shadow.

turret (TUR-et) A small tower, often containing a circular staircase.

vanishing point (VA-nih-shing POYNT) The place in a perspective drawing where parallel lines appear to meet.

Index

Web Sites

Due to the changing nature of Internet links, PowerKids Press has developed an online list of Web sites related to the subject of this book. This site is updated regularly. Please use this link to access the list:

www.powerkidslinks.com/htd/castles/